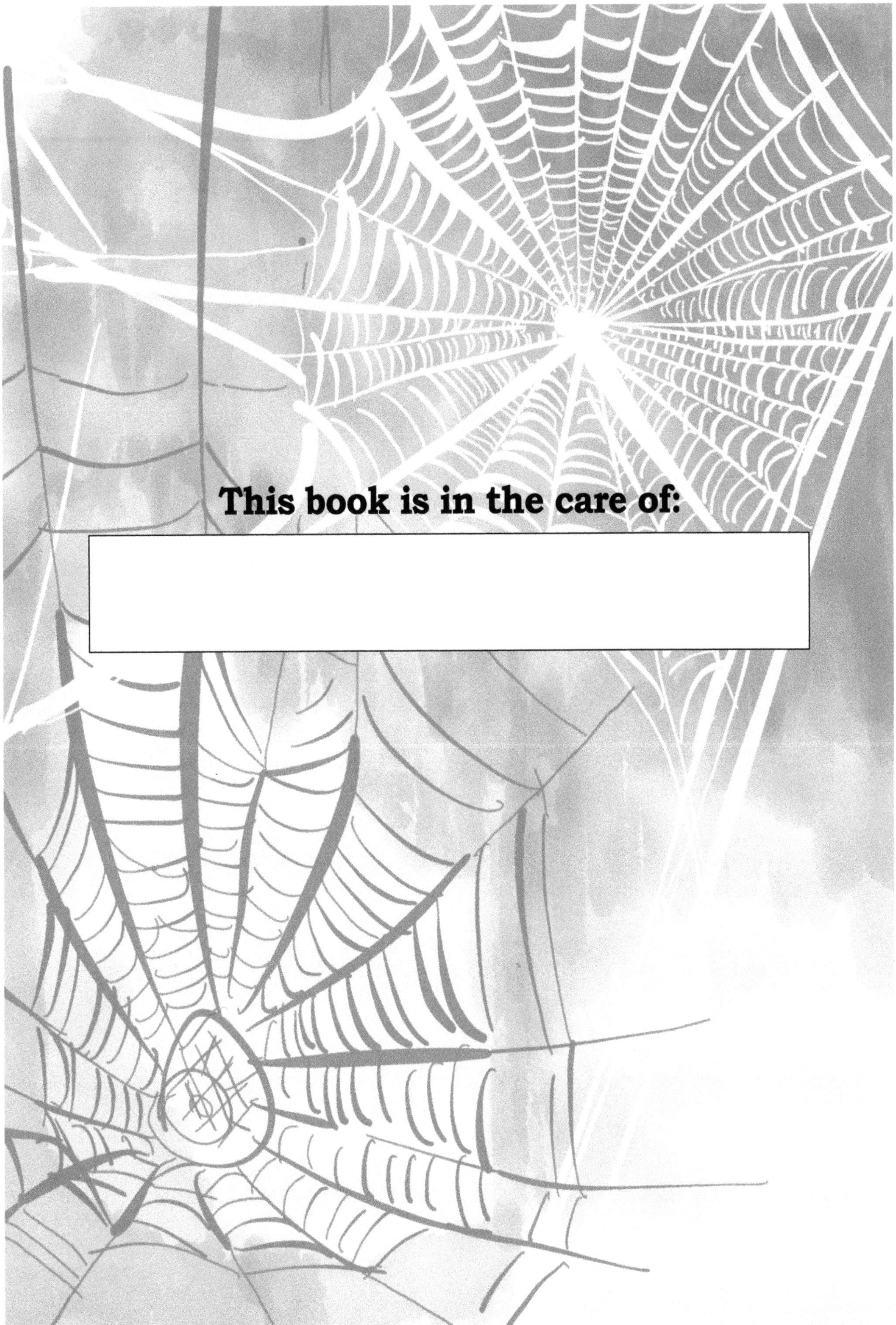
This book is in the care of:

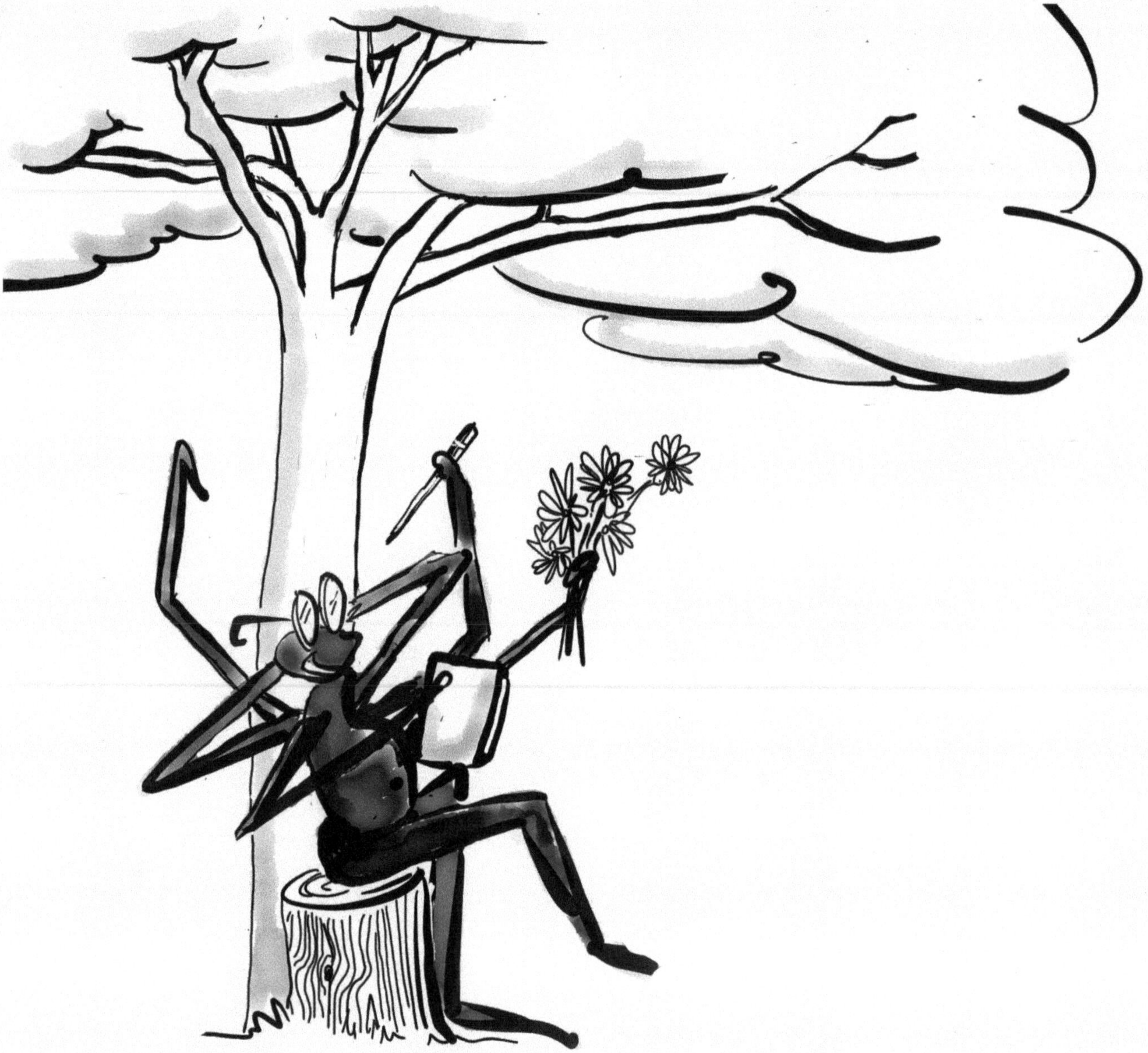

Thank you Melina
for the "paper" and "pencil"
and... I love you.

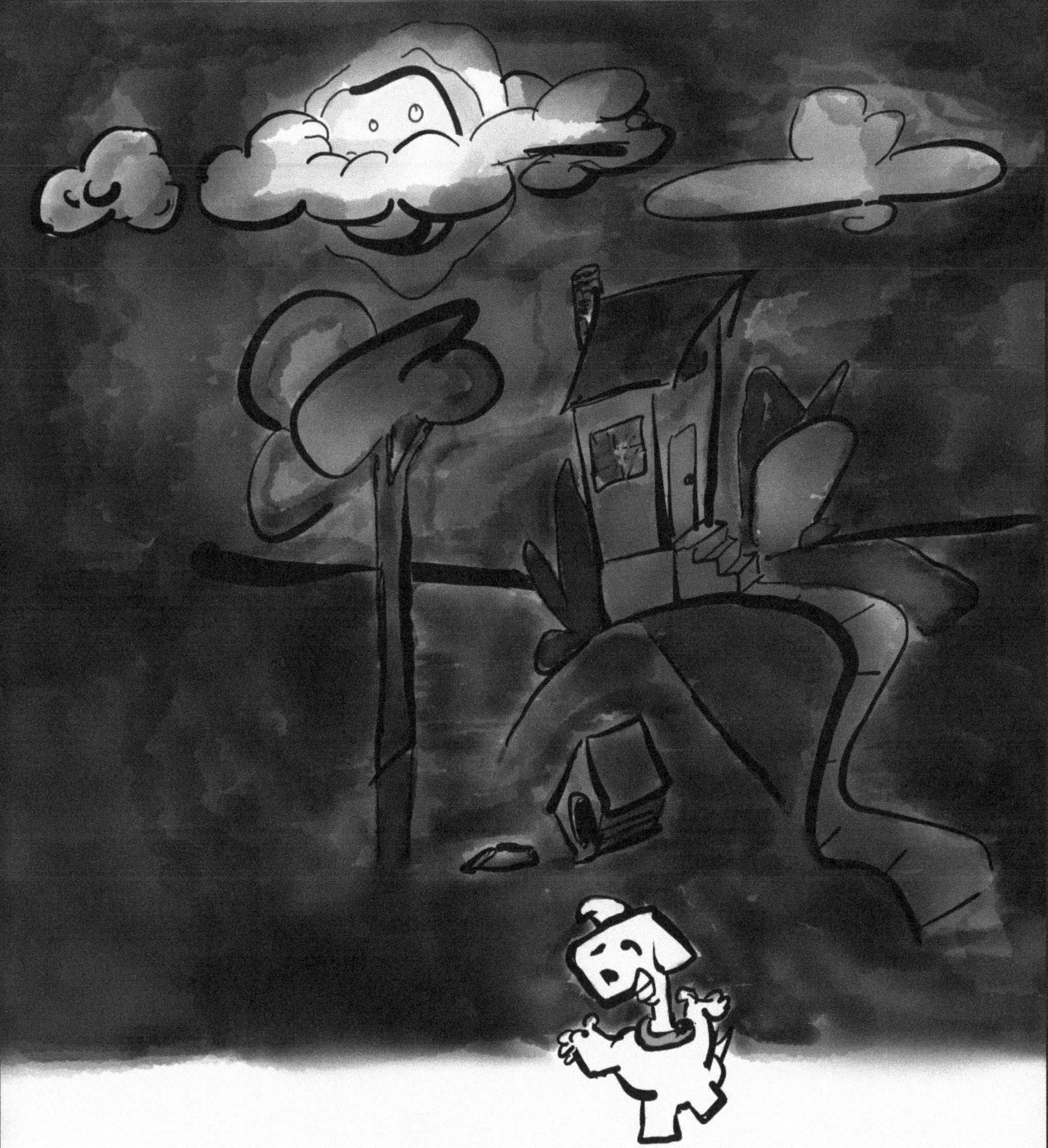

where do spiders go at night?
Do you think they are sleeping...
just because you turned out the lights?

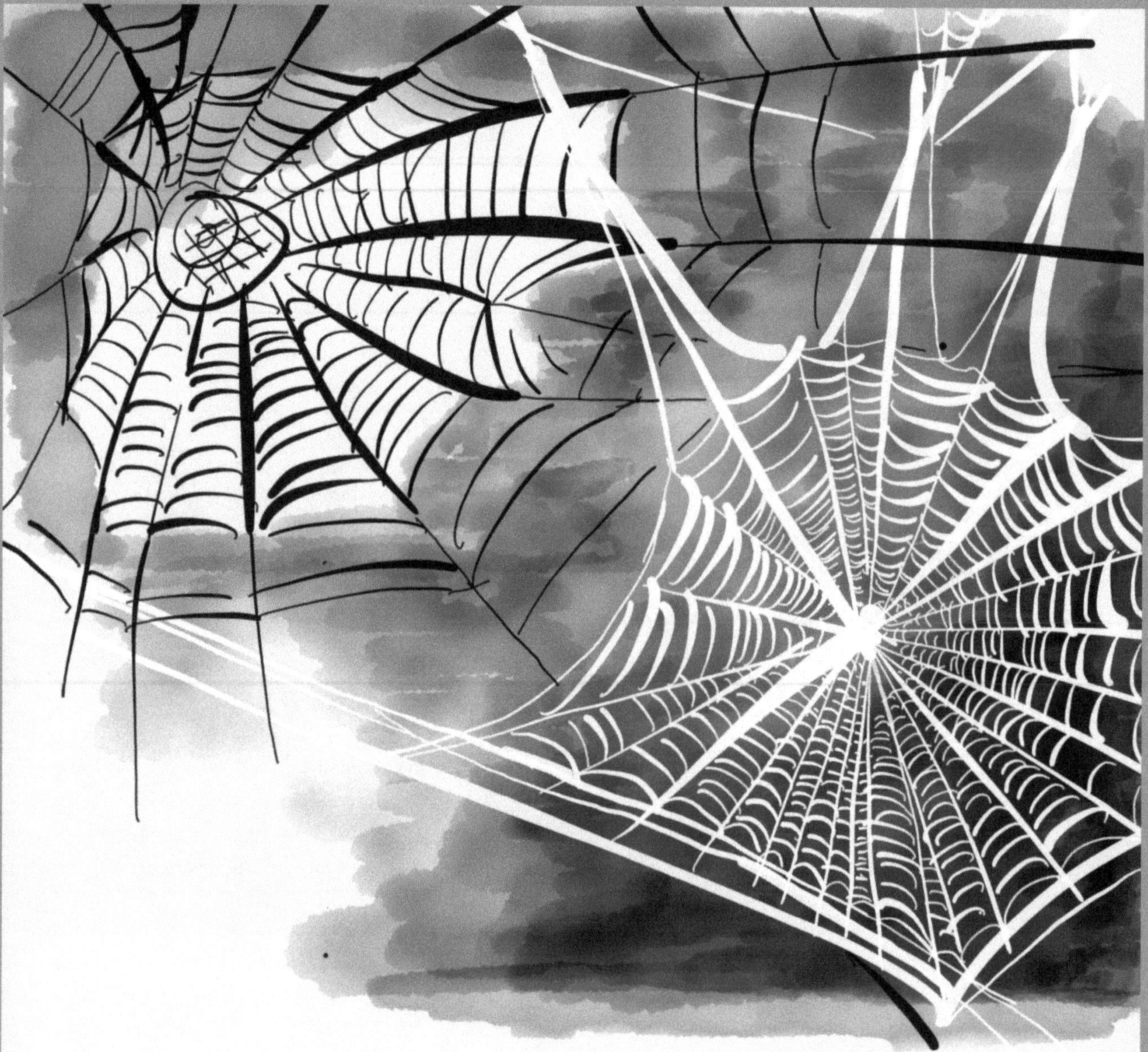

Spiders don't have webrooms for bedrooms.
So maybe they use yours?

Besides, it is cold and dark
and there are bats outdoors.

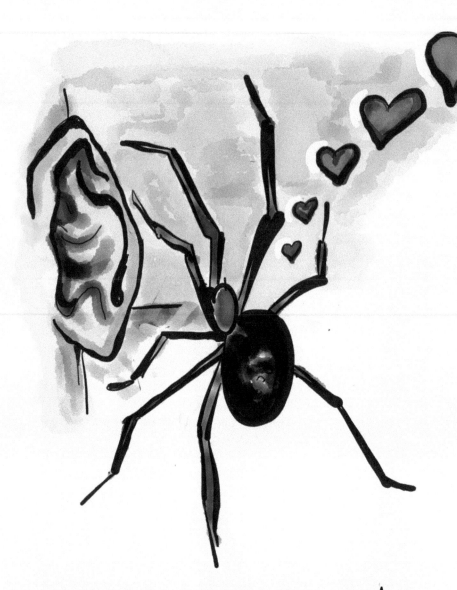

This may or may not
bring you to tears.
Spiders <u>love</u> your warm ears.

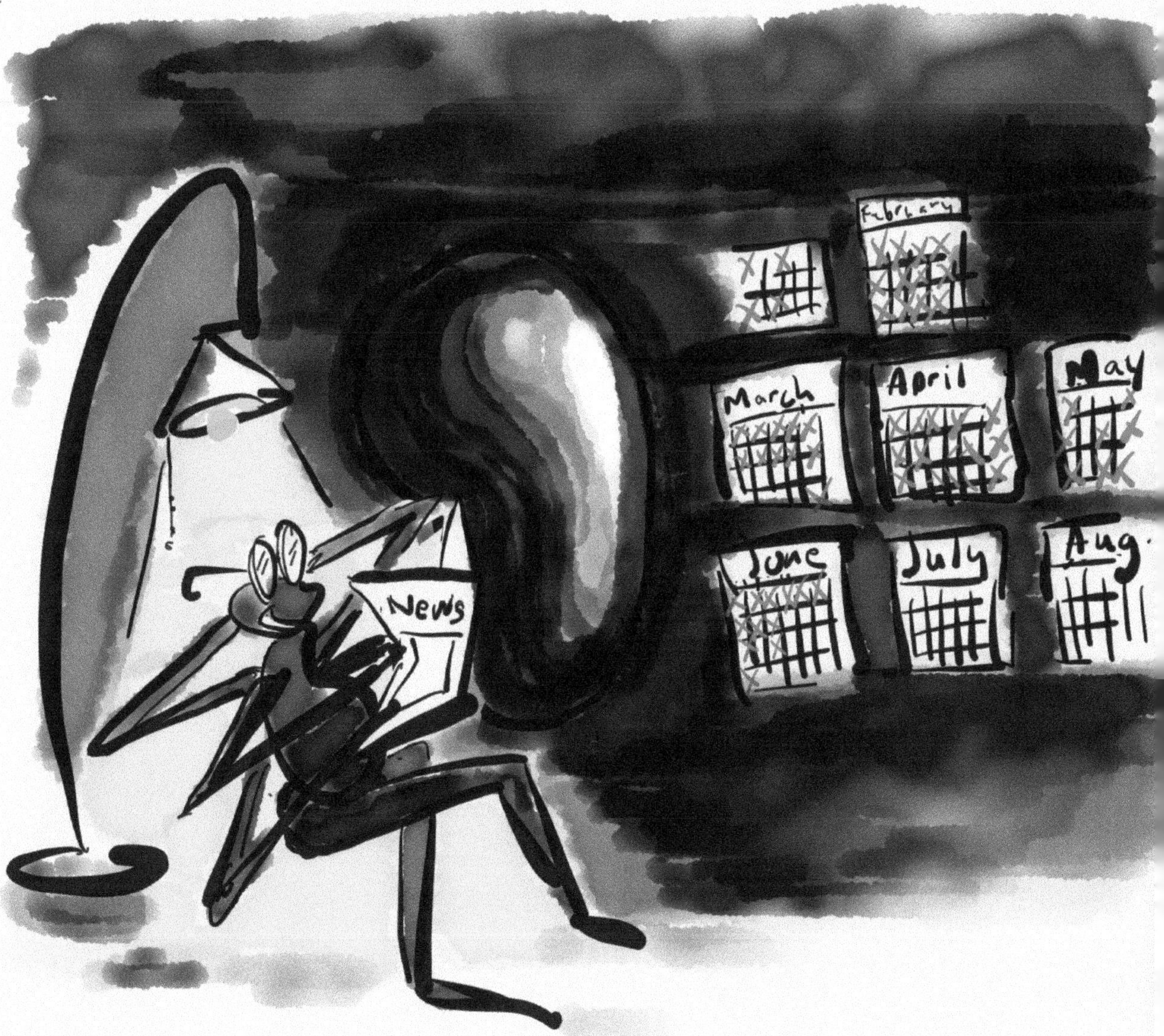

February
March
April
May
June
July
Aug.
News

They could get in there
and hide there for years.

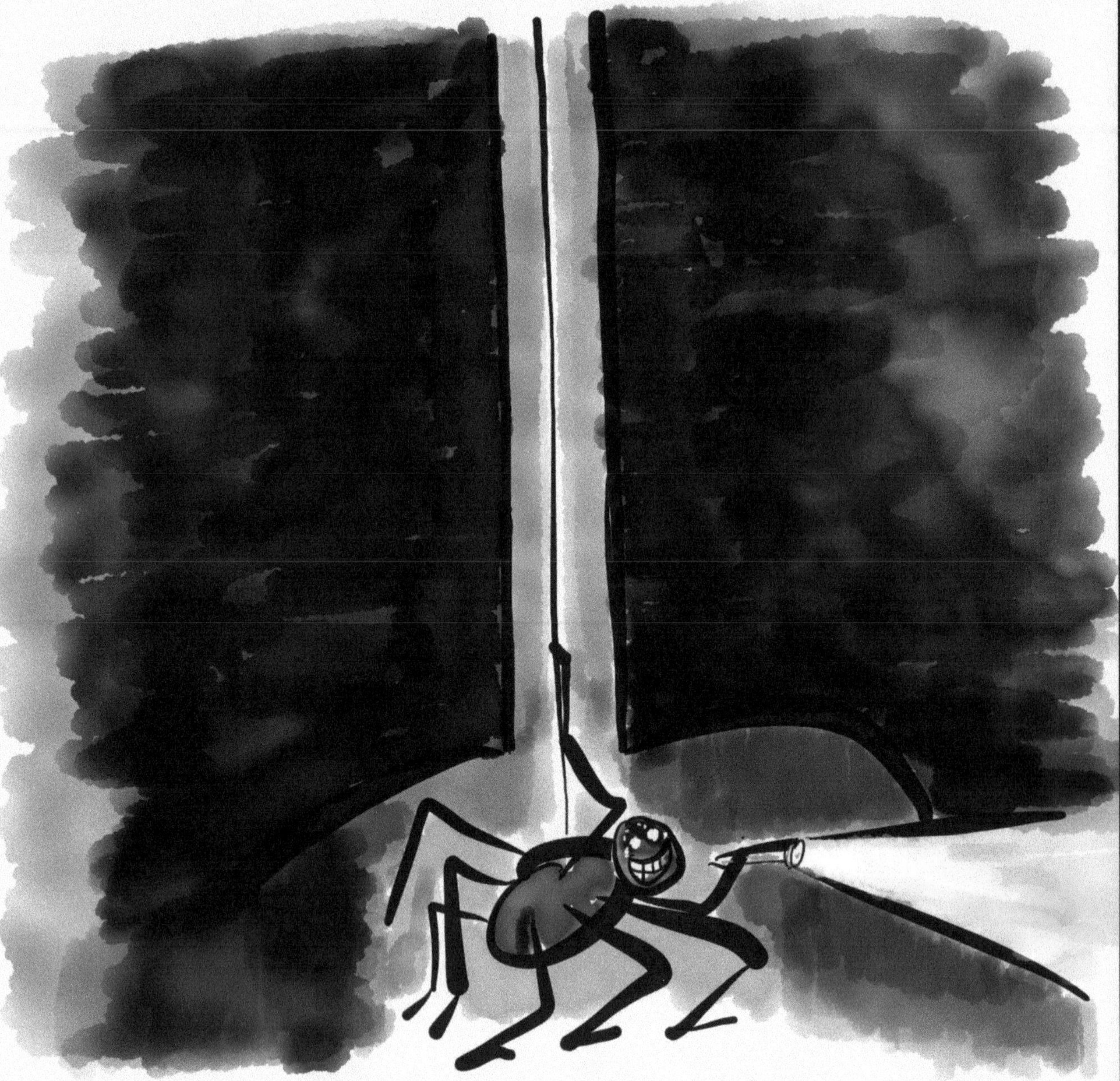

Dark and deep are these people caves.
Really the best place to misbehave.

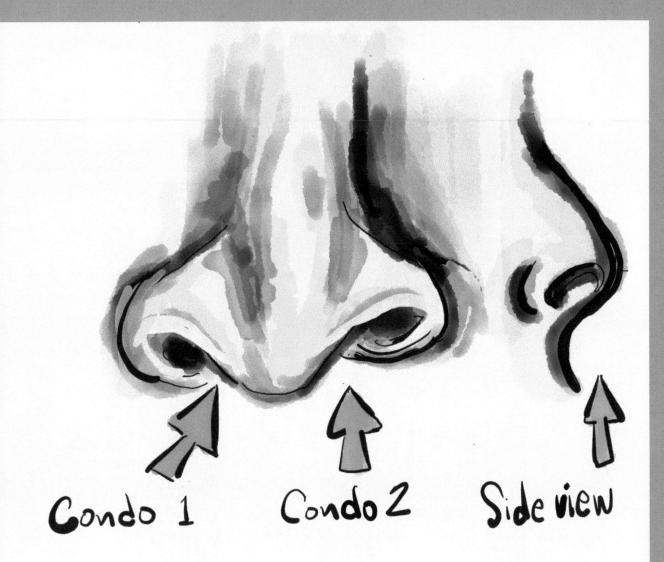

Condo 1   Condo 2   Side view

Nostrils, not everyone knows,
are little spider condos
right under your nose.

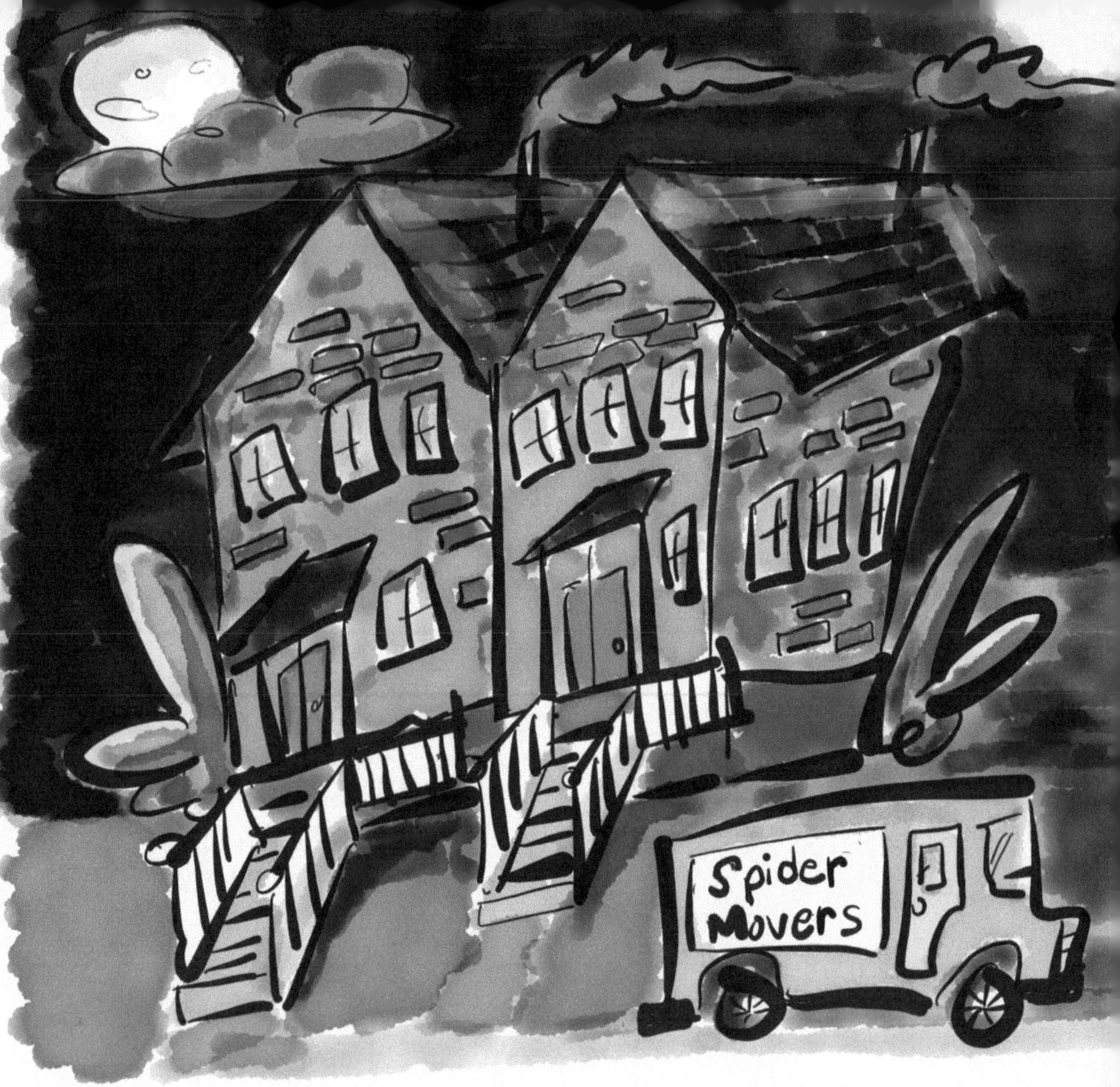
Spider
Movers

Not as complex
as a brick duplex
but two are built there,
Next to the next.

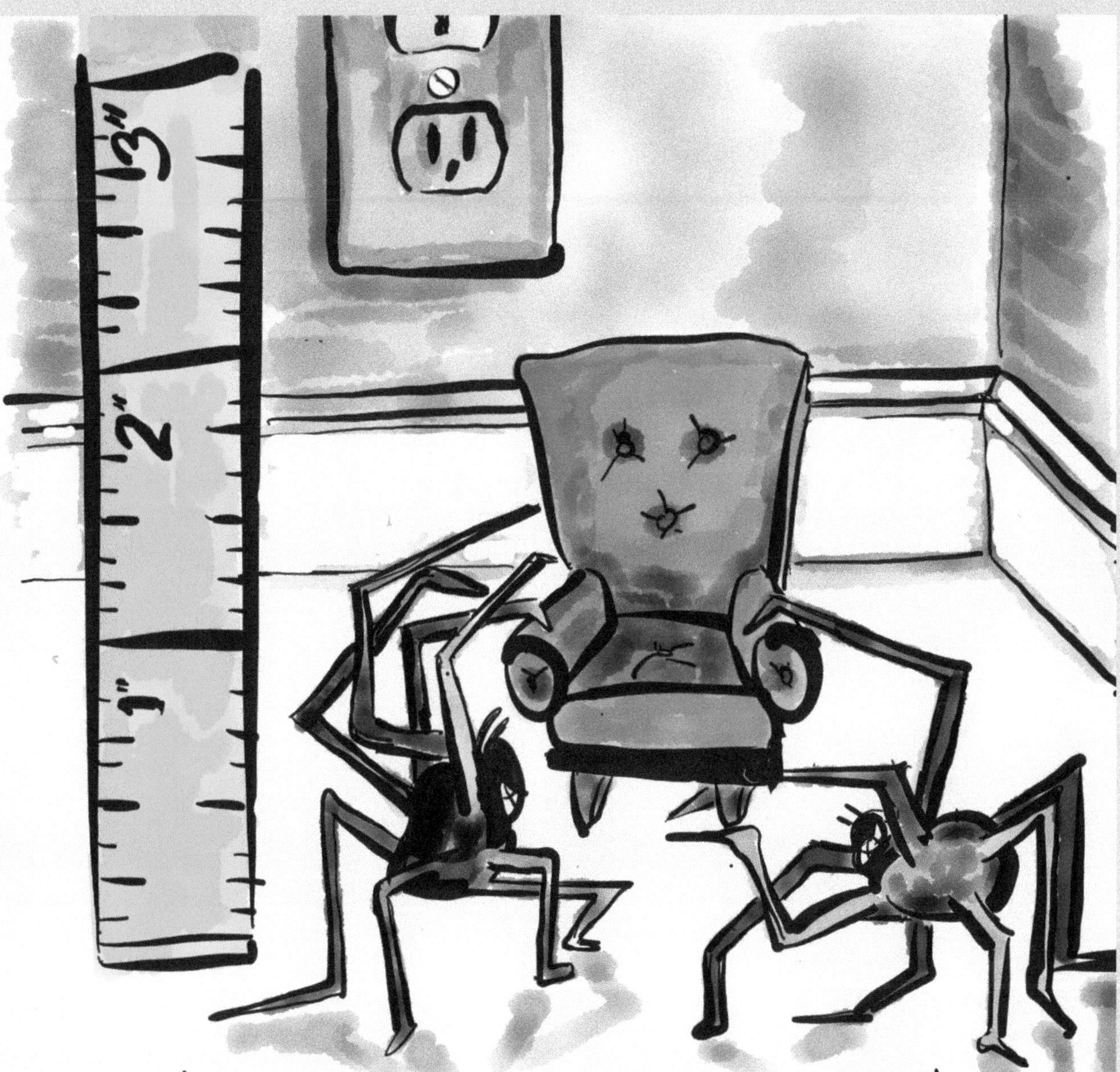
3"
2"
1"

And spiders are not very tall.
So moving in is not a problem at all.

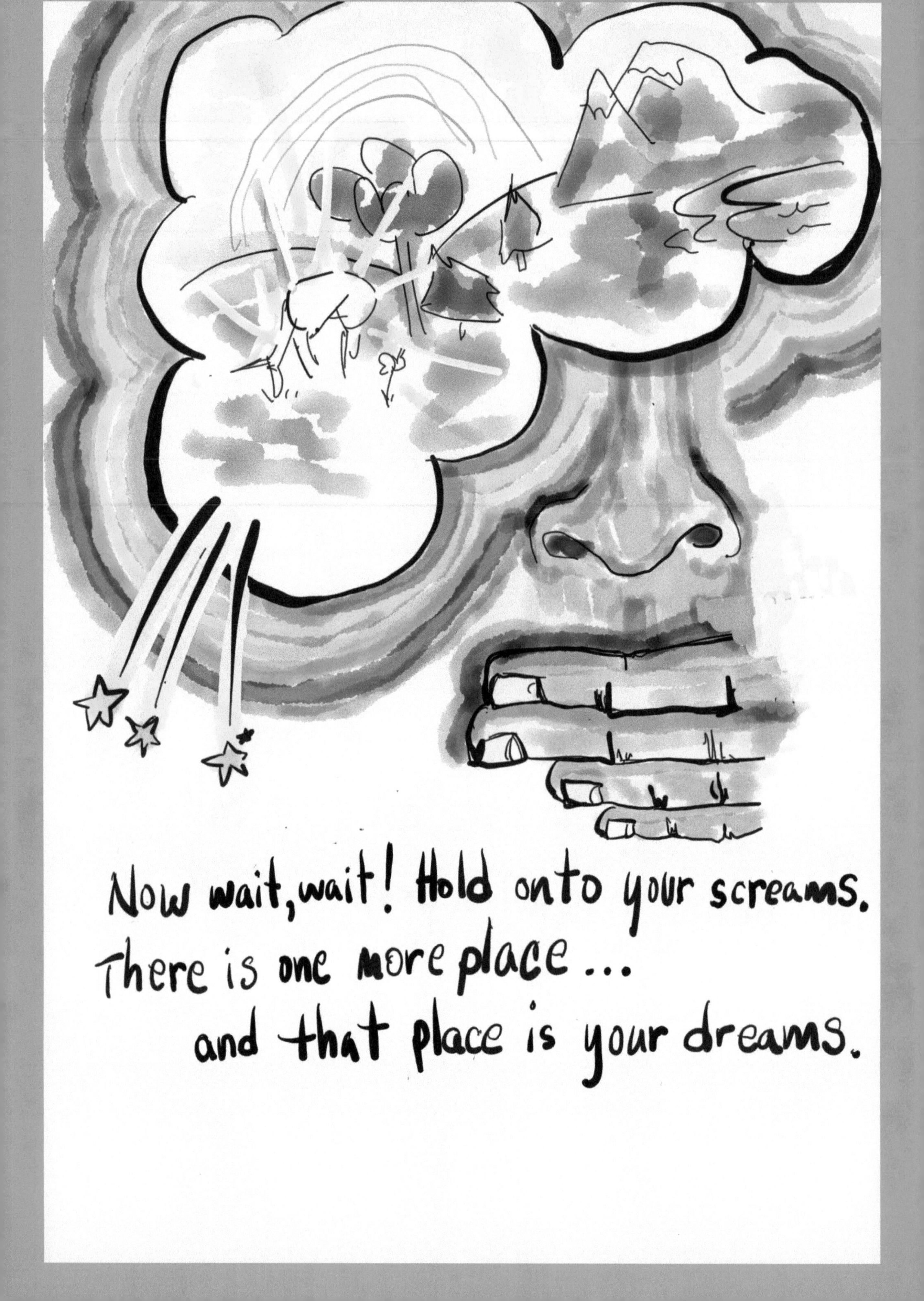

Now wait, wait! Hold onto your screams.
There is one more place...
and that place is your dreams.

Spiders get in using webs and eight legs.
Dreams are a great spot
to drop all of their eggs.

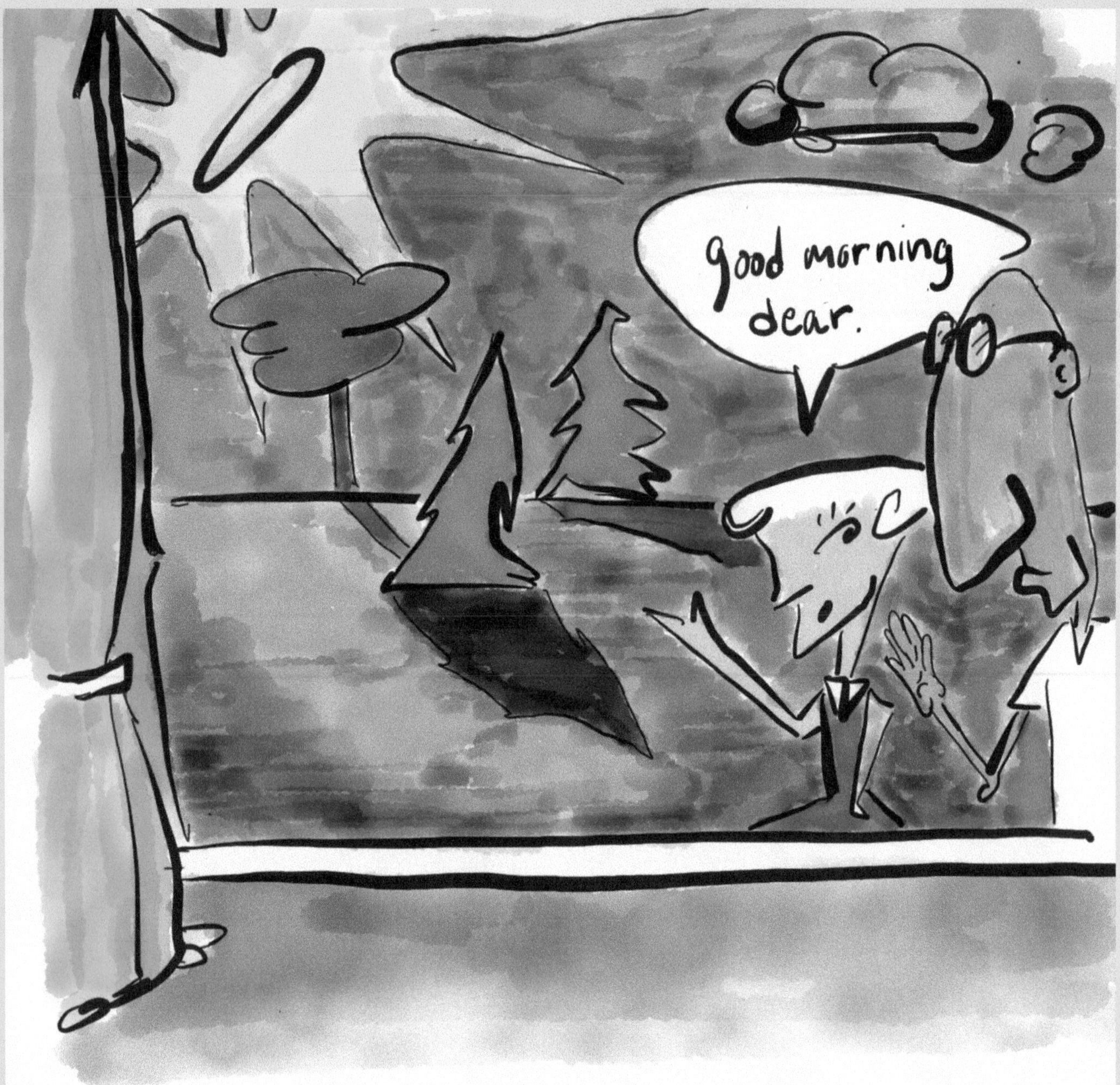
good morning dear.

It is now morning and the sun is shining in.
You scratch an itch beneath your chin.

To the bathroom you rush,
to brush your teeth again.
You look to the mirror,
to give it a grin ...

Your mouth is white and webbed shut!
Now you know for sure ...
where the spiders have been.

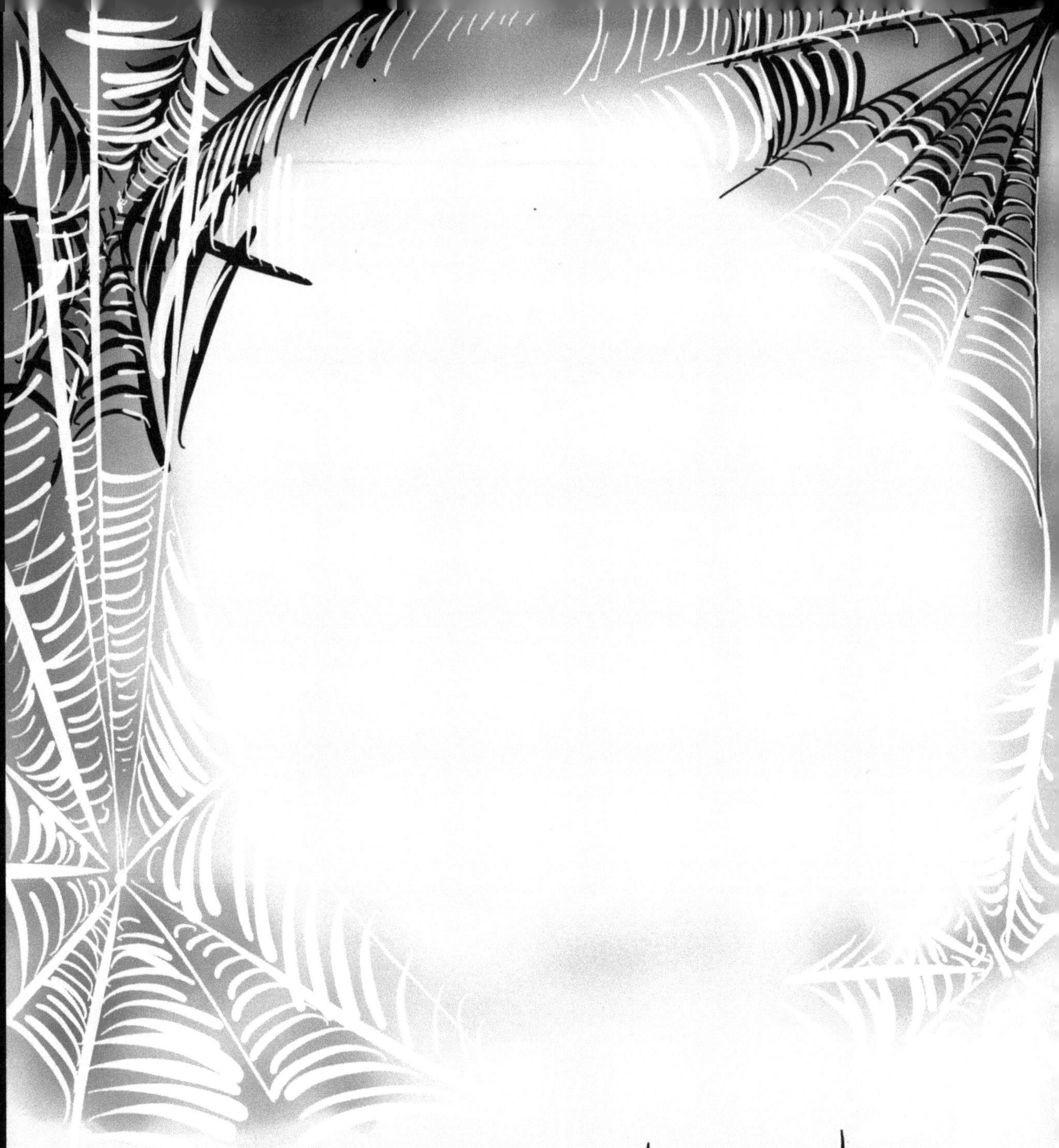

Here is some space to draw a place
for your favorite spider to hide.

No matter your age here is another page to show your imaginative side.

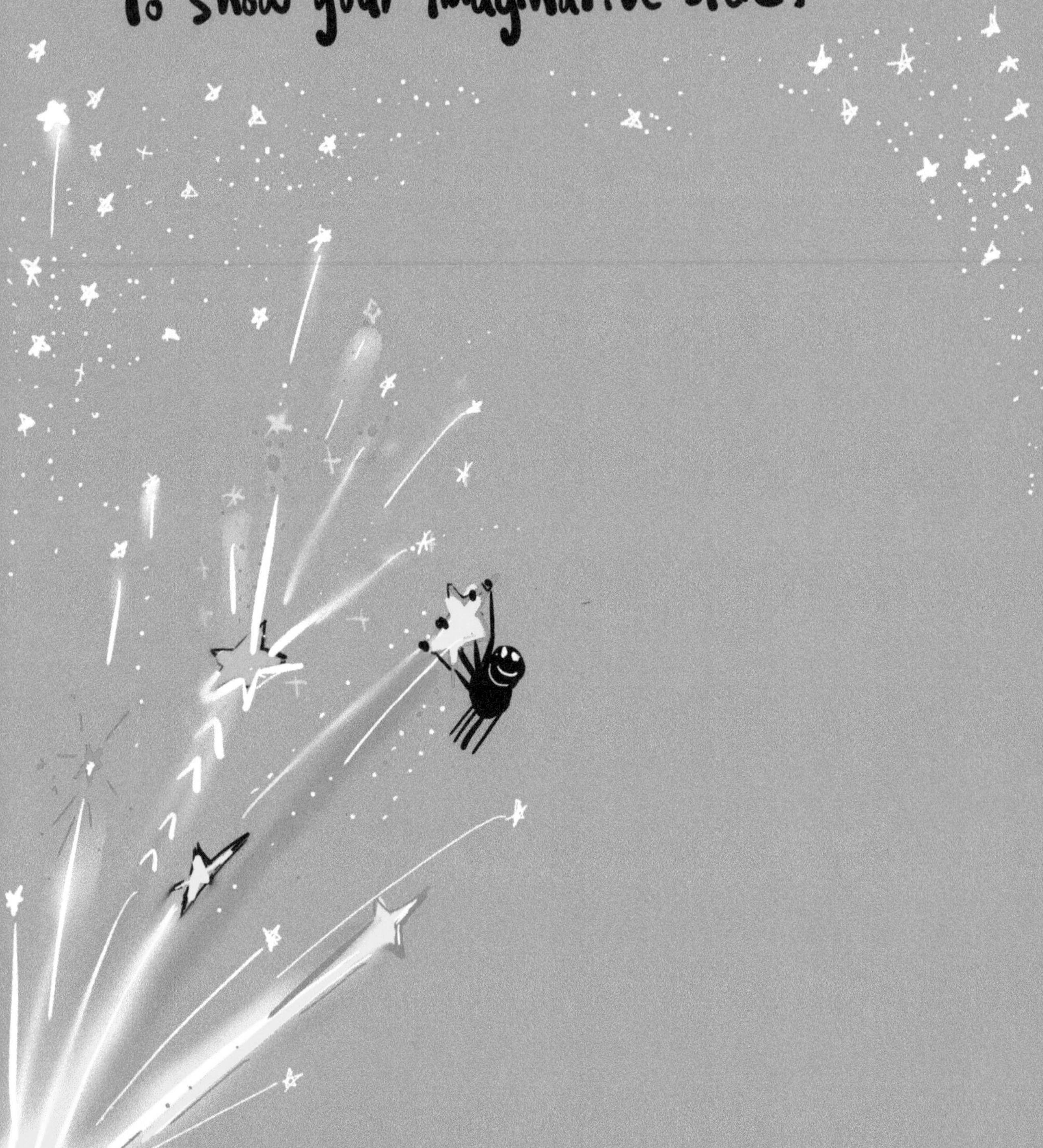

This is the last blank spot
for spiders to squat
and you can draw them skinny or wide.

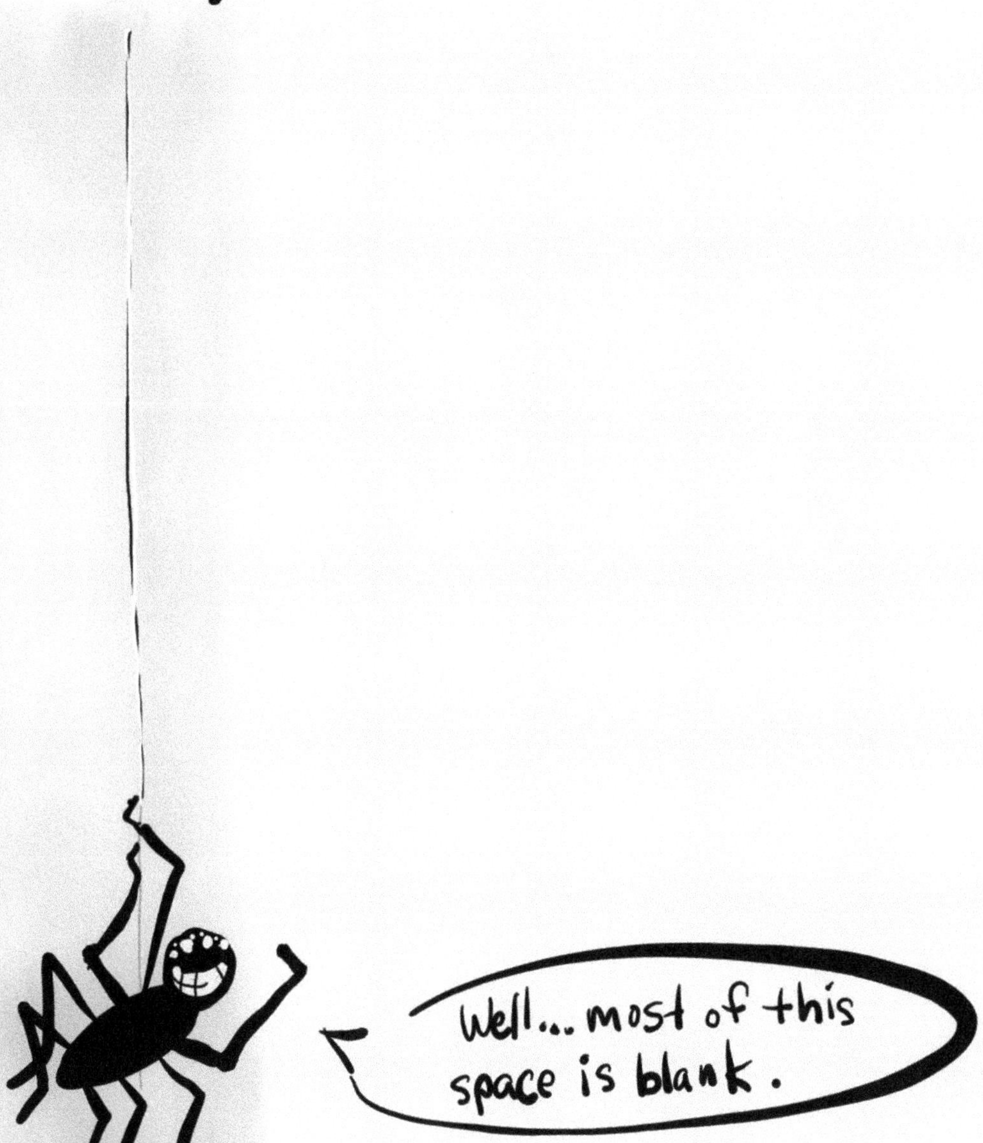
Well... most of this
space is blank.

the end...

<u>About The Author:</u>

Nick Gotelaere was born in Duluth, MN in 1971 and lived in Superior, WI. There are not many spiders there. When he was 12 he moved to Colorado, which has many more. He even lived in Hawaii for a few years and the number of spiders there are endless! He doesn't dislike spiders, and he hopes, you won't either. Please enjoy and thank you for this read.

P.S. The spiders said to say hi!

The Story of

Frida Kauai
publishing

To spread aloha, we hope you agree with giving our time and proceeds.
Helping our earth, our animal friends, and others in need.
Planting the 'Pay It Forward' seed.

Frida Kauai Publishing donates a portion of every publication sold to causes supporting our environmental, animal, and humanitarian welfare.

"One of the most charmingly illustrated books I have laid my eyes on! The story is so clever and imagination stirring! So happy to have found this new and super talented author and illustrator!"

- Tracy Franklin, someone with kids

"Usually I would be scared of spiders, but this story was fun and made me feel joyful! The illustrations are clever, detailed and exciting to look at. A favorite among my nieces and nephews."

- Carly Russell, someone without kids

"A clever beautifully illustrated read, perfect for parents and littles alike."

- Heidi Cuneo, someone with kids

"This book has just enough edge to it to keep me tingling through the pages! Fun, fast read and you'll probably grab a few q-tips when you are finished!"

- Dr. Taco aka Tommy, someone without kids

Published by Frida Kauai Publishing LLC

First Edition Copyright © Text 2019 by Nicholas A. Gotelaere

Copyright © Illustrations 2019 by Nicholas A. Gotelaere

Editing by Storm Williams & Susan Stokley

Identifiers:

ISBN: 978-1-7331831-4-7

Library of Congress Cataloging-in-Publication Data

Names: Gotelaere, Nicholas, Author | Gotelaere, Nicholas, Illustrator | Title: Where do spiders go at night? | Summary: A dusky yet colorful exploration of where our eight-legged friends like to go when the stars appear.

(LCCN) Library of Congress Control Number: 2019907877

LC record available at: https://lccn.loc.gov/2019907877

Instagram: @fridakauaipublishing #fridakauaipublishing

Our books may be purchased in bulk for promotional, educational, or business use. Please contact your local bookseller or Frida Kauai Publishing LLC Sales Department,

Fridakauai@gmail.com 720-381-2808

CPSIA information can be obtained
at www.ICGtesting.com
Printed in the USA
BVHW052204120819
555736BV00002B/2/P